Your House Cleaning Business, A Blueprint For Success

- ✓ Step-by-Step Guide
- ✓ Easy Start Up
- ✓ Get Clients Fast!

Wendy Williams

Copyright ©2015 by Wendy Williams

Imagine not dreading Mondays anymore!

Are you looking for a part-time or full-time career option that pays well and offers freedom and flexibility? Would you like to start a business that is simple, affordable, and easy to run? Would you like to own a business that is always in high demand, despite a "bad" economy?

Whether you're in between jobs, need extra money to pay bills or pay down debt, or have always dreamed of owning your own business, house cleaning is a service that is always in high demand and one that can quickly and easily help you reach your goals.

Be up and running in as little as two weeks, with a list of happy clients who will refer business to you again and again.

Learn:

- Why house cleaning for others is awesome
- The easiest, cheapest and fastest way to get clients, GUARANTEED!
- Why starting solo, without employees, is a great business model
- How to set rates and send quotes
- How to keep track of clients, appointments, keys and alarm codes
- The art of cleaning quickly and efficiently
- The truth of "natural" cleaning
- How to deal with difficult situations
- How to keep the word-of-mouth referrals coming
- How to easily show confidence and a winning attitude
- Why Mondays are Fun Days in this business!

Wendy Williams, also known as "The Cleanup Queen," has operated her house cleaning business since 2009. In Your

<u>House Cleaning Business: A Blueprint for Success</u>, she shares her real-world experience and down-to-earth advice with you in order to drastically cut your learning curve as you start your own cleaning business or improve upon the business you already own. She lives in Temecula, California, and loves going to "work" every day!

Table of Contents

INTRODUCTION

Why Would You Want To Clean Houses?

 I've always enjoyed cleaning and felt a sense of accomplishment in seeing a sparkling room that was messy or dirty moments before. Some people enjoy creating order out of chaos. Can you relate?

I always enjoyed cleaning houses on the side as I grew up and when I went to college. Even with a full-time job as a dental assistant, I continued to enjoy cleaning. The work paid so well and gave me instant gratification.

In my 40's, I was laid off from my executive assistant position. This was a blessing in disguise, because I decided to take more control of my own schedule and life.

I attended a few local business networking groups to get the word out about my cleaning services. I thought it would be a good idea for me to make some quick money cleaning until I found my next "regular" job, even though I dreaded the thought.

Luckily, I only had a couple of interviews at places I didn't want to work anyway, and it was then I realized that I really loved cleaning. It paid well and had great hours, and I decided to continue with it full-time.

That's how my business, The Cleanup Queen, was born, and I've never looked back. After 6 years, I'm still cleaning, and don't dread Mondays anymore.

Over the years, I've talked with a number of women who want to know more about starting up their own cleaning business.

Most of these women are "in

transition," where they've recently been laid off, are newly single, or just don't know what they want to do next. Some women are stable, but need some extra money to help with the bills or pay off debt.

Cleaning can be the perfect "in between" gig, or even a permanent full-time career, like mine. Startup costs are very low, and most people already have the basic skills to start.

Still, there's a learning curve to this whole cleaning thing. That's why I decided to put everything I've learned into this guide, in order to help you get your first paying clients in as little as two weeks! I wish I had this book when I started.

What about you? Do you feel stuck in a 9-to-5 job, wanting more freedom over your own schedule? Have you recently been laid off, or are you going through a divorce? Do you need money soon and don't know what to do next? Maybe you just need some extra income to help with the bills? Perhaps you're a student who needs good pay and a flexible schedule to work around your classes?

Whatever the reason, you've come to the right place to get your business off to a quick start. And the best part is that you'll get paid every day you work. No waiting for a paycheck!

This book is more than a mere pep talk. It's also more than a dry, boring manual on the details of business ownership. I don't cover business mechanics or how to grow a huge company with employees and subcontractors. Nor do I cover how to write a business plan or secure a bank loan.

This book is designed specifically for the solo operator wanting a simple, no-fuss business with very low overhead and minimal hassles.

If that's why you're here, I won't let you down.

I even show you the exact emails I send to my client when providing quotes and raising rates. I give you the exact phrases I use when I meet potential clients, words that work!

Whether you want a side stream of income or want to go full-time to enjoy the freedom and flexibility of having your own business, you'll get plenty of good advice and actionable steps in the pages to follow.

Think of me as your mentor. I'm happy to share everything I've learned over the years so that you can succeed as well!

I would love to hear from you. Reach me at wendiki@sbcglobal.net.

Wendy Williams

"The Cleanup Queen"

www.TheCleanupQueen.com

Let's get started!

STARTING OUT

House Cleaning is Awesome!

I could go on and on about why I love this business, but the main reason is that I'm my own boss. I like me as a boss and I'll bet you'll like yourself as your own boss, too.

With your own house cleaning business, you'll get to work as often or as little as you want. You don't have to ask your boss to take time off when you want to visit relatives, go to the doctor or dentist, or take a vacation.

Of course, you'll notify your clients when you need to reschedule or skip a cleaning for whatever reason, but they're usually gracious and understanding. Most of your clients will value your services so much that they won't mind when you take an occasional day off or need to reschedule.

You'll enjoy a very attractive hourly wage at $25-$45 per hour as compared to most entry-level and retail jobs at $10-$12 per hour.

And you'll get paid every day! Talk about instant gratification. When is the last time you were paid at the end of each day's work?

You'll be home by 2:00 or 3:00 most days, leaving time for you to pick up the kids from school, do homework, or whatever else you want to do.

You'll enjoy the varied work environment. In the corporate world, I dreaded going to the same place at the same time, day in and day out. Now I get to see a different house or houses each day, and I'm there for only 2-3 hours each. It's great.

But most importantly, you'll get immediate satisfaction from your work. I enjoy knowing my clients love coming home to their fresh, clean, sparkling house!

Qualities of a Happy House Cleaner

You certainly don't have to love cleaning to enjoy the benefits of your own house cleaning business. As long as you don't hate cleaning, you could find the work enjoyable, given the many benefits.

I love a good makeover, don't you? We love to see a frumpy woman transformed into a knockout, or a drab messy room turned into a space worthy of a spread in Better Homes & Garden.

Cleaning someone else's house is a similar experience. Unlike many conventional jobs, you get instant personal satisfaction along with smiles and praise from your happy clients.

But cleaning is physically demanding. You'll need to move quickly, and there's lots of kneeling to clean low and hard-to-reach places, hiking up and down stairs, scrubbing, vacuuming, and bending over to move and pick-up items. You'll work up a sweat with all the activity. I've always said I don't need a gym with all the activity I do in my line of work!

Are you honest? People are letting you into their homes, so they must trust that you won't steal anything or be so careless that you're always breaking things. Eventually you'll have plenty of word-of-mouth referrals, which calm those fears before they even meet you. Until that time, references or letters of recommendation will help a lot, and you'll learn more about those later.

Do you pay attention to details? Many of my clients say they didn't even notice that an area in their home was dirty until I cleaned it. Sometimes it's the crevice of a cupboard door or a cobweb up in a corner that I've cleaned. It's clearly obvious to me, such as cleaning the outside base of a dirty toilet that a client's previous cleaner never touched. If you notice details, you'll have happy clients.

How are you at communicating with others? While you don't have to be Miss Congeniality, you do need to step outside of your shy shell a little bit, enough to smile and exchange pleasantries when you meet your clients, and to keep in touch with them via phone, text or email.

You should be moderately organized and self-disciplined. Are you usually on time or running late? Can you usually find your keys, sunglasses and phone right when you need them, or are you chronically misplacing them, also causing you to run late?

Do you wake up in the morning easily on your own, or do you need prodding to get yourself out of bed after hitting the snooze button three times? Missing consultations or cleaning appointments and not being on time are a sure way to build a bad reputation.

Be honest with yourself. If these things are a struggle for you, you may struggle in this business. But if this is important to you, you can begin now to change some of these habits, making yourself more magnetic and successful in this or anything you want to achieve in life.

Starting With As Little As $20

 This is a person-to-person business, and the very first thing you must buy are business cards to hand out to people you meet. They'll see you, they'll see your nice card, they'll be impressed, and they'll hold onto it – I guarantee it. So if you buy nothing else, make sure to get your cards!

I use www.Vistaprint.com . 500 cards cost $10 plus an additional $10 for standard shipping, and I get them in about 7-10 days. I get compliments all the time on my cards, and it's a stock image. The standard cards use vibrant colors on high quality paper, so they make a good first impression. The Vistaprint website is easy to navigate and they make it simple to customize your cards.

Naming your business is important.

Jot down a few name ideas and ask friends and relatives for feedback or for their ideas. It can be as simple as using your own name, or getting creative with words that evoke "clean" imagery. Have fun with it.

When getting your business license, you can save the cost of filing a Fictitious Name Statement, or DBA (Doing Business As) by using your own surname. For instance, if your name is Suzie Crane, you might name your business *Crane's House Cleaning.* Check with your county clerk, though. If you need to file a DBA, there's a small cost for filing the name with the county clerk, as well as running a special business notice to the public in your local paper for several weeks (the clerk will give you instructions on how to run the notice).

The cost for a business license can vary from $25 per year to well over $200, depending on your location.

Run a Google search "Business license (your city)" for licensing information.

Google "Fictitious Name Statement (your county)" for filing a DBA.

You'll need to choose a business entity. Again, run a Google search "choosing a business structure" to read an excellent article by the Small Business Administration to help you decide. There are legal and tax consequences for whichever structure you choose. I like the simplicity of being a sole proprietor, but you need to carefully consider what's best for you. Pick your business structure before filing for your business license and purchasing liability insurance.

Regarding cleaning products and supplies, I recommend you purchase and use your own, but that will take about $100-$150 to start. It's well worth it, though, because you know which products work best and make your job easier, plus you can charge a premium for your services. But it's not required. Most clients are happy to provide the products you need and request if you can't or don't want to bring your own.

Two car magnets from www.Vistaprint.com for about $30 were also a great investment for me. Neighbors of my clients saw my car with the magnets and thought of me when they needed a cleaner. I landed 2 clients by using them, earning me over $3,500. Nice return.

But if you only have $20, business cards are a must. Keep them in your purse and in your car, and hand them out freely.

Insurance

No one likes to talk about insurance, but we must.

Most people aren't clear what "insurance and bonding" means for cleaners, and this is a very brief overview.

Please consult with an insurance broker, who will be happy to fully explain everything and give you some options that will work for you.

Here goes:

General liability insurance protects your business from someone else's claim of bodily injury, associated medical costs and damage to property. If your client slips and injures himself on the floor you just mopped, you're legally liable for the injury and associated medical costs. Or if you break a client's crystal vase, for example, you are liable.

A bond is commonly known as "employee dishonesty" insurance and protects the client against theft or loss by you.

I don't recommend starting a cleaning business without insurance and bonding; however, I did not have it for the first 5 years of my business. The cost was prohibitive for some reason where I lived in Northern California.

When clients asked if I was insured and bonded, I was honest and said, *"No, I'm not, but only because it's so expensive. I'm very careful, though, and I can provide you with letters of recommendation from my clients who would be happy to speak with you to ease your concerns."*

Most of the time, they would say, *"Oh, that's okay."* Because my business is built on word-of-mouth referrals, they're already pretty sold on me before I even give them a quote. Still, I think of how risky that was.

Most insurance companies offer payment plans, and I recommend you call an insurance broker to help you secure a good general liability policy and bond. If it's too expensive, you may choose to build up your client base when you're first starting out before purchasing a policy. But I'd recommend setting up a payment plan if possible.

When I moved to Southern California in 2014, the cost of general liability insurance dropped dramatically in my new location, and I bought a policy immediately. I believe the bond was the same in both locations at $100 per year.

Now I proudly tell everyone that I'm

bonded and insured. I don't wait for them to ask, and I use it as a marketing tool to help earn a potential client's trust. I believe this has helped me secure many new customers in my new location, so it's easily paid for itself.

Once you have insurance, make sure to state that on your business card, too.

SHOW ME THE MONEY

How Much Can You Earn?

 Since the business model I'm talking about here is simple and involves only you as a solo business owner, with no employees or subcontractors, your income is limited only by the number of jobs you can physically handle.

Most of my jobs fall in the $89-$119 range and take between 2-3 hours each.

So if you take on two jobs a day at $89 each and work 5 days a week, you would earn $890 per week and will usually be finished by mid-afternoon once you get the hang of cleaning efficiently. In this scenario, you would earn $3,560 per month.

Of course, your earnings may be more or less.

If you only need to earn a little extra income, you could take on just four jobs per month, spacing them out perhaps one per week, at $89 each to earn $356. That may be just enough to provide some financial stress relief.

The best part about this is the high hourly rate. You can earn quite a lot in 2-3 hours, especially compared to most non-skilled jobs that pay minimum wage.

Of course, you'll need to set aside funds from your gross income (total income before taking taxes and expenses into account) if you're using your own cleaning supplies and equipment.

And never forget to set aside money for your taxes! I can't stress this enough. You'll need to figure the amount due and the payment schedule of quarterly (or estimated) taxes on your own or consult with a qualified tax professional. The IRS doesn't fool around with what's owed to them, so make sure to plan accordingly.

Be smart and always set aside money for your supplies and taxes.

What to Charge Your Clients

This can be a tricky part of the business. I recommend charging by the job, rather than by the hour. I've been cleaning long enough that I usually know how long each job will take and charge accordingly.

But how do you get to the point of knowing what to charge in the first place? Besides a fair dose of trial and error, which will happen, there are some guidelines you can use to help.

I first tried to find out what other cleaners in my area charged, but that was difficult. Obviously, they don't want to share that information with competitors.

I was able to ask some friends what they were charged, and that was a good start.

Large cleaning companies clearly charged much more than I could as a solo operator. They have higher overhead and also use teams of 2-4 cleaners. Some solo cleaners charge so little, they are lucky to be earning minimum wage.

You'll want to fall somewhere in between, not charging outrageous big-company prices, nor the lowest in town.

Here are the general guidelines I use today for bi-weekly cleanings (every other week):

- $79 for small homes up to 1500 square feet with 1 or 2 bathrooms, 1.5 hours to clean

- $89-$99 for homes up to 2500 square feet that are pretty clean with 2.5 bathrooms, up to 2.5 hours to clean

- $109, $119, $129 for homes up to and no larger than 3200 square feet, no more than 3.5 bathrooms, up to 3.5 hours to clean

These prices are based on a fairly clean house, minimal clutter, one pet, 2-3 people living in the house.

You should adjust these prices upward based on a number of other factors such as:

- More then 3-4 people living in the house

- More than 2 pets

- Lots of clutter and high levels of dust (dusting takes the longest of any task)

- Lots of furnishings, especially if they're crammed into small spaces

- Lots of dusting blinds

- Lots of mirrored closet doors or louvered doors

- Hard floor surfaces that need to be vacuumed and then mopped (taking twice the time as just vacuuming carpet)

- Clients who expect or request special cleaning tasks

These are general guidelines. I might charge $109 for a smaller house if it's packed full of stuff and has pet fur everywhere. These houses take longer to clean and I charge accordingly. The more people that live in a house, the dirtier it becomes, too.

I also have a few clients who like monthly or "occasional" cleanings. For these, I do not provide a quote, but rather charge a 3-hour minimum at $115. I let the client know that I work down their priority list. So depending on how much they have "picked up" and ready for me, I can get quite a lot of cleaning done in 3 hours. If I have the time available and they want me longer than 3 hours, I charge $35 per hour thereafter. Sometimes the houses are in great need of cleaning, and only the kitchen and 1 or 2 bathrooms get done, but I've never had a disappointed client afterwards. They're thrilled to have such a thorough, deep cleaning in the areas that they find the toughest to clean!

Bonus Tip: Before visiting a client's home to give a quote, type in their address on Zillow.com to get the square footage and bedroom/bathroom count. This will give you a general idea of your bid price before you even arrive. Once there, look around to see if your estimate is on target or if you need to make any adjustments.

For instance, I was recently called to give an estimate on a fairly new 2400-square-foot home. I figured I'd charge about $99 based on square footage and bathroom count. When I arrived, the place was very cluttered, with 5 furry, shedding pets running around. Nothing I couldn't handle, but I quoted $129, knowing it would take extra time, and they happily accepted.

Do not reveal your quote or your fees to the client when you're there. Let them

know you'll need to calculate the cost and then send an email quote. You'll learn more about sending out a quote later in the book.

Charging an Initial Cleaning Fee

Unless I'm cleaning an absolutely immaculate home, I always charge what's known as an "initial cleaning fee" for the very first cleaning. No matter how fast you think you can clean a home, it always takes much longer the first time. I allow 6-7 hours.

You're there to whip the house into shape and get it ready for subsequent "maintenance" cleans.

I usually charge an extra $125 "initial cleaning fee" on top of the regular fee for the first visit.

When you're first starting out in the cleaning business, everything takes longer. You may not even get to everything in 6 hours, especially if it's a large home. Just explain to your client that you will get all the basic cleaning done, and some of it will get cleaner as you go for the first several visits.

The initial cleaning is the best time to make a good impression. Pay attention to the details and be thorough with everything. It's a good feeling, knowing your clients will be elated with their sparkling clean home.

THE CLEANUP QUEEN'S SCHOOL OF CLEAN

Cleaning 101

If you aren't starting out using your own supplies, consider setting aside a few bucks from each job right away so you can buy some to make your job easier and faster on future cleaning assignments. You can charge your clients a higher rate when you bring your own supplies.

You don't have to buy your own vacuum cleaner; however, I highly recommend you invest in a small, lightweight professional canister vacuum. I just love my Sanitaire by Electrolux Mighty Mite. It's been one of the best investments I made in my business.

You can always use your client's upright vacuum for rugs and carpet, but those never work well for cleaning hard floors or even carpeted areas under beds and in small, difficult-to-reach places.

I eventually bought my own upright vacuum as well, and I use it on a few homes, the ones with really bad vacuums or none at all. Yes, some of my clients don't even own a vacuum! My Shark Navigator Pro upright vacuum is light, maneuverable and really picks up all the stuff, including pet hair, from rugs and carpets.

My mid-size car with a standard trunk is just large enough to hold all of my cleaning supplies. But I keep my upright vacuum on the back seat of my car on top of a towel since I can't fit it in the trunk with everything else.

The mop and vacuum attachments are kept in the trunk floor on an angle in order to fit in. I also bought a two-compartment collapsible trunk organizer for $20 that holds all of my towels, cleaning cloths, microfiber mop pads and replacement vacuum bags. It keeps everything organized and in its place.

A small box holds my extra cleaning solutions and supplies that I may need to replace between jobs.

I manage to carry everything from car to house (except the upright vac) in one trip, too. I carry the canister vacuum's removable wand, mop and bucket handle in my right hand, and the small canister vacuum itself on my hip (between my right arm and hip). My left hand holds the cleaning caddy. Takes a little practice, but it sure saves time going back out to the car again.

Efficient Cleaning

Speaking of time, let's talk about cleaning efficiency. Since you're cleaning "by the job," and not by the hour, you'll want to become more and more efficient. When I first started and was cleaning by the hour, I quickly realized that I was cutting my own paycheck drastically the more efficient (faster) I got. The house was getting cleaner and cleaner in a fraction of the time.

So when you clean by the job, the opposite will occur; the faster you get, the more your "hourly rate" goes up, and you'll be able to take on more work. And you'll get faster, without sacrificing quality, over the course of the first several cleanings at each client's house.

The reason it takes most people so long to clean their own homes is because they are simply not efficient. That's why we professionals carry a cleaning caddy from room to room. We maximize our time upstairs before moving downstairs, and we're not wandering from room to room getting distracted and wasting time. This all comes with time and practice as well as mental preparation.

I had a client who told me it took her 2 hours to clean her master bedroom and bath before she hired me and was amazed that I cleaned her entire home beautifully in the same amount of time.

When you start out, you'll be significantly slower than even a few months later. At the end of each cleaning day, take a mental review of what you did and think about how you can work a little faster without cutting corners.

My cleanings are like a daily movie in my mind as I review each room, and I think of ways I can shave off time without sacrificing quality. Even when I'm on my way to an assignment, I mentally go through the house wondering how I can do a better job in less time. It works!

Of course, there's a point that you can't cut more time and still maintain top quality. For me, I reach peak efficiency in each home after about 3-4 cleanings.

So make it a fun game to see how you can continually improve your cleaning process, in a shorter amount of time, in each home.

Supply List

I started out from the beginning with my own supplies, but you can always start out by having your clients provide you with the basics at first.

 You can purchase almost all of these items at Walmart or Target or even Amazon. Walmart doesn't carry Mrs. Meyer's products, but Target does. Also, you can buy the LA's Totally Awesome cleaner at Dollar Tree.

Here's a list of what I bring to each job:

- Plastic cleaning caddy with 3 compartments

- A 2-gallon bucket with a sturdy handle

- Several white terry cloth wash cloths

- Several microfiber cloths

- An old bath towel

- Pumice Stick (for cleaning rings and heavy accumulation inside toilet bowls)

- Blue no-scratch scour pads

- Green heavy-duty scour pad (don't use these anywhere except the inside of the toilet bowl)

- Toothbrush or small nylon detail brush

- Natural all-purpose cleaner such as Mrs. Meyer's. I buy the concentrate and mix with water in a professional-grade spray bottle.

- Playtex Living Gloves

- Ammonia-free glass cleaner

- LA's Totally Awesome All Purpose

Cleaner and Degreaser

- Soft Scrub with bleach

- Lime-A-Way

- Bar Keepers Friend cleanser

- SprayWay Stainless Steel polish

- Furniture polish

- Swiffer dusters

- Steel wool soap pads

- Small plastic rinse cup

- Webster (or other cobweb brush on an extension pole)

- O-Cedar Dual Action Microfiber Flip Mop (with removable microfiber pad)

- Sanitaire Mighty Mite canister vacuum (for hard floor surfaces, upholstered furniture, under beds, and any areas that an upright vacuum can't reach)

- Shark Navigator upright vacuum (for carpet and large area rugs)

In the cleaning caddy, you'll keep:

- Glass cleaner

- LA's Totally Awesome cleaner

- Mrs. Meyer's cleaner

- Lime-A-Way

- Soft Scrub

- Bar Keepers Friend cleanser

- Toothbrush or detail brush

- Plastic rinse cup

- Green scrubber

- Blue scrubber

- Steel wool soap pad

- Pumie Scouring stick (pumice stick)

In one of the small compartments in your caddy, or within a little container in your bucket, keep the green scrubber, the pumice stick and a toothbrush – all for toilet work – separate from everything else. You don't want these germy items cross-contaminating anything else!

In the 2-gallon bucket, you'll keep:

- Terry and microfiber cloths

- Gloves

- Swiffer duster

- 1-3 microfiber mop pads

- Furniture polish

- Stainless steel polish

- Anything else that may not fit in your cleaning caddy

Remember to refresh all your supplies between clients. Throw away scrub pads after each cleaning assignment, and thoroughly launder all terry and microfiber cloths and mop pads before using them again.

I keep a small box of quart-size freezer bags and a permanent marker in my trunk. I don't want to throw away a partially used pumice stick after one use, so I slip it into a bag with the client's name so I can use it the next time I clean their house.

Warning: Before you begin, read all product labels and instructions. You are responsible for the safe and proper use of every cleaning product you use!

Some chemicals can cause permanent damage to household items. As a professional, you are required to understand precisely how to properly and safely use each product.

Repeat this process whenever you use a new cleaning product.

Virtually every home I clean has damage somewhere due to the incorrect use of a cleaning product. Toilet bowls are damaged from highly caustic toilet bowl cleaners that were left to sit for too long, etching the enamel. Or the same cleaner was spilled on the vinyl floor and left to sit, causing permanent and unsightly damage.

I also see scratched stainless steel appliances because someone used a heavy-duty scouring pad or scouring cleanser on it.

Most common are ruined fiberglass and porcelain tubs and showers from the use of scouring cleansers, scouring pads and even phosphoric acid products that were left on too long in an attempt to remove hard water deposits.

Again, read each label carefully so that you have a full understanding of each product's safe and proper use.

For further information on product safety as it relates to your health, visit www.MSDS.com.

Risky Business: A Word about Bleach

You may be wondering where the bleach is on my cleaning list.

First, bleach is NOT a cleaner, but is a powerful oxidizer. You can spray bleach all day on soap scum, greasy stove tops and so on, and get nowhere.

However, in the shower or tub area, a small bit of Soft Scrub used with a small brush will take care of any mold or mildew that may accumulate in the corners or on grout. You can also try a 50/50 diluted water/vinegar solution to kill mildew in these areas.

Bleach, if mixed with ammonia or other cleaning chemicals, can create a toxic – even deadly – chloramine gas or vapor. It's extremely dangerous to breathe!

Hospitals and large institutions use bleach as a disinfectant, but residential homes are sanitized by simply using regular cleaners and a cloth or paper towels. The only area in a home that may require bleach is a cutting board that's had raw meat on it, and house cleaners are not expected to clean those.

Another problem with bleach is that it will cause permanent damage to rugs and carpets if any leaks out of the bottle or splashes out. I've heard nightmare stories where this has happened to other house cleaners, so I just don't use it. I recommend you don't use it, either.

Bleach is not a cleaner, and the potential damage to your client's home is too great.

Now for the fun stuff. Let's talk about getting your first clients FAST!

MARKETING MAGIC

Two Weeks to Your First Clients

If you want to start earning money right away, and with good quality clients (and who wouldn't?), then you'll need to get in front of people to build likability and trust. Yes, face-to-face time is required. But don't worry, it's not difficult, it's not forever, and I'll show you exactly what to do so it's much less intimidating.

> The best way to quickly get serious, quality clients who value your skills is to get referrals by attending business networking meetings.

Don't get "networking" or "business networking" confused with "network marketing" which is related to multi-level marketing (MLM). This is something completely different, and they are not even related to each other!

I had a successful cleaning business in

Northern California for almost 6 years and recently moved to Southern California, 600 miles away and had to start over from scratch. I didn't have any clients lined up and certainly needed income right away.

What you're about to learn, step by step here, is exactly what I did to get my first paying clients in just two weeks. Within 3 months, my calendar was full. I did it, and you can, too.

My goal right now is for you to get paying clients as fast as possible, with minimal cost and hassle, so you can build momentum and start earning money almost immediately. Then you can experiment with multiple forms of marketing if you wish.

Let's talk more about networking meetings or "networking groups" and why I think they're the most efficient and fastest way to get your cleaning business started NOW.

Business Networking 101

Let's first go over what a networking meeting is.

These meetings consist of a group of 10-30 people that meet once a week at a restaurant, over a meal, for the sole purpose of sharing their business and building relationships. This, in turn, helps everyone get new business in the form of referrals.

I'm sure you've caught yourself saying, *"If I had a dollar for every time I've told so-and-so about XYZ, I'd be a millionaire!"* You just gave that person a personal recommendation, or a referral.

I know the idea of attending a meeting with a room full of people that you don't know can be scary and intimidating. I'm here to explain everything about a meeting, even what to say and do, to lessen the unknown and give you confidence – and get clients fast!

What's unique about these network meetings is that they are "category-specific," meaning there is only one member per business category allowed. In other words, there is only one real estate agent, one chiropractor, one auto mechanic, one massage therapist and so on. Sometimes exceptions are made when categories have two separate branches, such as a residential real estate agent and a commercial real estate agent. In my group, I was the residential cleaner, and a fellow member was a commercial cleaner.

In a networking group, a referral (also called a "lead") is a recommendation to give business from one person to another. You may get referrals not only from people within the group, but members may also refer you to other people that they know from outside of the group.

These meetings are built on recommendations, or "referrals" of business each and every week. That's a powerful and fast way to build your business!

Members usually become a close, tight-knit group, and they freely refer business to one another because of one proven business principle:

People do business with other people they know, like and trust.

People who don't know you really can't get a sense of whether they like or trust you by looking at a flyer, website or your card on a community bulletin board. Consider adding these strategies to your marketing plan later on, as time and money allow. For now, remember:

- Paid advertising costs a fortune and doesn't work quickly.

- Leaving cards on community bulletin boards is somewhat effective over a long period of time, but oftentimes the potential clients are only interested in having you come in for a one-off cleaning at dirt-cheap prices.

- Flyers are expensive, time

consuming to distribute, and attract more "tire kickers," or people who want a cheap, one-time cleaning.

- A website can be very valuable, but you don't need one right away to get your first clients.

But right now, you absolutely need to get yourself in front of people, face to face, to establish that likability and trust. It's the *most important* thing you can do to win people over and get them to hire you immediately.

That's why attending these networking meetings is highly effective. You'll reap the rewards very quickly, and hopefully make some new friends and have a good time, too!

How Networking Meetings Operate

As I mentioned, most groups meet at a local restaurant over a meal, and most meetings are held very early in the morning – not all, but most.

When you walk in, you'll notice a

bunch of tables grouped together to create one large table or seating area.

You may be greeted by someone and asked to sign in. Don't panic! Smile, introduce yourself, and tell them what you do. They're happy to have you there – really!

After about 15 minutes of gathering, socializing and casual networking, the president will ask everyone to take a seat so the meeting can get started. Take a seat and quickly decide what you want to eat from the menu, as the server will be around quickly. Then around the table, each person has a chance to stand up, introduce themselves and talk about their business for 30-60 seconds.

The meals will be brought out while people are talking, and there's no need to wait. Dig right in and listen while you eat.

Around this time, a small file box containing every member's business cards will be passed around. Take one of each. The president, at some point, will also let you know when you, as a guest, can pass around your stack of cards. Make sure to come prepared with at least 40 cards.

Guests will have the chance to introduce themselves and talk very briefly about their business after all the members have had their turn. Again, don't panic! The next chapter goes over exactly what I say at this point in the meeting, and you can adapt it to fit your needs and personality.

At this time, a featured member will give a 10-20-minute presentation on their own business, followed by questions and answers. It's a good time to learn more about that person. Don't be shy during Q&A, and ask them a question. It shows that you're confident, even though you're a new guest. People love to do business with confident people!

Here's where we get into the heart of the business networking meeting – REFERRAL TIME! Each member will be encouraged to share three things:

1. Say something they liked or enjoyed about the meeting

2. Share a recent positive business transaction within the group

3. Give referrals, written out on referral slips provided

Around the table again, each member and guest will stand up and share these three things.

Don't worry if you don't have any referrals to give; you won't be expected to since you're a guest. But you should always say something positive such as, *"Sue, your presentation was terrific, I learned so much about (whatever they presented). What a friendly group! I'm interested in learning more and would like to attend again."*

Members will also go around and share something positive about the meeting, followed by any "wins" or positive business transactions with other members, such as, *"Cindy gave me the best facial last week, I can't wait to get another one next month!"* or, *"Todd, I really enjoyed getting to know you better over coffee last week."*

Finally, each member will give out referrals on referral slips, saying something like, *"Mary, I am in desperate need of house cleaning, so I need you to call me so we can talk about your rates and get a quote,"* or *"Mary, my sister just told me her house cleaner moved away and she needs a new one! Here's a referral with her information on it, so give her a call."*

Remember, this is all done quickly, with each person getting about a minute to share all three things: What they liked about the meeting; any successful "wins" or business transactions during the past week; and any referrals they want to give.

Now the meeting ends after the president makes any last-minute announcements and thanks everyone for being there.

Members and guests often linger for a

few minutes to socialize or talk more "business," and a membership committee leader may even take you aside to ask if you have any questions about the group and even encourage you to join.

Meetings always begin and end on time, as business owners need to get back to work. These groups mean business, literally, and are very effective at building good referrals and business contacts.

This may seem intimidating, but I've given you a really clear picture of what to expect, which should lessen your fear. I didn't know a thing about these meetings when I first walked in, alone, and more than a little nervous. But I just wore that smile, put on my confident face, and did just fine. I left feeling encouraged and enthusiastic! You will, too, and you'll be amazed how everyone loves to have a house cleaner in their group.

When it's Your Turn to Talk

Have a 30-second presentation – often called an elevator pitch - ready so that when you're called upon to introduce yourself during the meeting, you're not stumbling over what to say. Here are a few variations of what I say:

"Hi, I'm Wendy Williams, also known as The Cleanup Queen. You hate house cleaning. I love it! Call me."

Or

"Hi, I'm Wendy Williams, The Cleanup Queen. Do you really like cleaning toilets? Are you really eager to catch up on cleaning chores on the weekend? If not, I'm here to help!"

Or

"Hi, I'm Wendy, The Cleanup Queen. My ideal referral today would be a retired couple, not yet ready to downsize, who needs help with the overwhelming chore of keeping their house clean."

Here's a variation... *"My ideal referral today would be a young couple with children who need an extra hand cleaning so they can concentrate on being the best parents they can be."*

I've used this phrasing with minor variations, and I always get smiles and nods, because most people there know of someone in that situation. They WANT to give you a referral, so this is a great way to jog their memory of who they know who may need your services.

Over time, you may also choose to give a great cleaning tip to change things up and keep yourself and others from hearing the same thing over and over.

For instance, one time I said, *"Hi, I'm Wendy, The Cleanup Queen, residential cleaner. Most people dread cleaning out the toilet bowl, but I've got a magic secret right here in my hands,"* whereupon I bring out a brand new, clean pumice stick. *"Put on your gloves, get this pumice stick wet, and scrub away that built-up hard water ring. Don't use acid bowl cleaners, use this non-toxic miracle cure! I'm Wendy, The Cleanup Queen."*

Well, everyone loved it, and they all

wanted to know where they could purchase a pumice stick and had lots of questions for me after the meeting. Some members prefer to do their own housework or already have a house cleaner, so they'll appreciate your cleaning tips. Eventually, they may hire or refer you because you've clearly demonstrated your cleaning know-how.

More Meeting Tips

- Arrive 10-15 minutes early. "Pretend" you're the greeter, and walk up to those just arriving, shake their hand, and introduce yourself. This is more comfortable than walking into a room full of people, in my experience. Tell them you're new and that you're happy to be there. You'll make a great impression!

- Bring 40 cards in your pocket or purse. Keep them readily available so you're not fumbling when you need to give out your card.

- Dress "work appropriate." Most people will be there in the clothes they typically wear to work. I wear jeans, a print top and flats. I don't want to wear my actual cleaning clothes, so I step it up a notch.

- Consider wearing a magnetic-backed name badge. They're so much nicer than the paper stickers they provide with your name scribbled on with a marker. I bought mine from Amazon for $15, or you can get one from your local printer. You can also wear it when you meet clients at their homes to give quotes. You'll stand out in a positive way with a nice name badge.

- Be enthusiastic and happy. Even if you're tired or grumpy, you can put on a cheerful face for an hour to get new business and make a positive, lasting impression. The best part is that you'll feel good after each meeting, even if you walked in dragging your feet.

Following Up After the Meeting

Hopefully you have a whole stack of new business cards from all the members of the networking group. When you get home, review them all and make notes on the back or attach a sticky note to each. The magic is in the follow-up.

Email everyone you spoke to and received a card from. People are so pleased with an acknowledgement and friendly word or two. I've made many new friends and associates this way. I usually write something simple like this:

Hi, Joan!

Just wanted to say "Hello" and tell you how nice it was to meet and speak with you at today's networking meeting. What a great group – so friendly!

I would love to get together with you over coffee soon, if you have a few minutes, just to get to know you better.

Fridays are best for me, but let me know what works for you.

Looking forward to seeing you again soon!

Wendy Williams

The Cleanup Queen

(my phone number)

Almost everyone writes back, thanking me for reaching out and being so friendly, and many times they will throw out a few possible dates to meet for coffee. It's a wonderful, casual way to get to know people better.

Does Networking Really Work?

I've never been to a networking group yet where I didn't get at least one referral for cleaning business, even though I was there for the first time as a guest. I'd say that's worth it.

I can't guarantee this will happen for you, but this is how I began building my client base in just 2 weeks after I moved to a brand new town 600 miles away, starting completely from scratch. This worked so fast, I was truly thrilled with the results.

Be positive, follow up quickly on referrals, and watch your business grow. Always be confident and proud that you're a house cleaner. Remember, you're providing a valuable service that people need to make their lives better!

How to Find a Networking Group

This is pretty easy, especially if you live in or near a larger town or city. Here's a list of the ways I recommend finding a group or groups near you:

1. Run a Google search "business networking groups (your city)".

2. Call your local Chamber of Commerce to ask for a listing of business networking groups in your area. Even if you're not a member of your Chamber, they are happy to help you. Take advantage of this great resource!

3. Search Meetup.com, under "networking" and "business networking" in your area to potentially find even more groups.

4. Finally, call a few nearby small business owners and ask which networking group they may attend or know of. Most real estate and insurance agents attend them, as well as mortgage lenders, window washers, pool maintenance people, computer repair technicians, auto body and repair shops, accountants, attorneys, and other solo and small business owners.

Here are few well-known business networking groups.

- BNI

- LeTip

- Trusted Business Partners

- TEAM Referral Network

Try a Google search such as "BNI (your town)" or "LeTip (your town)" and so on.

Once you have your list of groups, call each chapter leader to introduce yourself and ask if you may attend. As long as they don't have another residential house cleaner in their group, they'll be thrilled to have you and will even pay for your meal.

If they hesitate, it's because they may have a commercial cleaner already in their group, which may pose a conflict. Remember, these business networking groups are category-specific.

This happened to me once. I simply asked them to talk to their commercial cleaner and assure them that I would only promote my residential cleaning business.

In this case, the commercial cleaner was happy to have me, and we've since built a good referral base for one another. Whenever I get requests for large commercial or move-in or move-out cleanings, I refer those people to him. And since he doesn't clean houses, he always refers those people to me. It's been fantastic!

Women's Business Groups

Before my calendar completely filled up with client appointments, I also supplemented my networking group meetings by attending two different women's business groups. These are not "category-specific" and are open to all. In other words, it's common to see several people from competing business categories, such as real estate agents, financial planners, massage therapists, and so on at the same meeting.

The purpose of these meetings is similar to business networking meetings, except they are solely for women and are designed to encourage and uplift fellow members, personally and professionally, as well as educate them through featured guest speakers. Ultimately, through building good relationships with one another, the goal is to give business to one another.

I've never been to a women's business group that's had another house cleaner, probably because these meetings are held during the lunch hour, when most house cleaners are busy working. When you're first starting out and don't have a full calendar yet, attending these groups is worthwhile. I've secured several excellent clients by attending just a few times.

I found two women's groups in my area by Googling "Women's Networking Groups" and "Women's Business Groups."

Some groups will allow you to come indefinitely as a guest, paying a slightly higher attendance fee than a paid member. Some groups will allow you to come twice as a guest before requiring membership. Even if you can only come once or twice, it can be worth the many quality contacts you'll make by giving a great impression.

The two that I've attended cost $25 as a guest, which included lunch. Members pay $20, but also a yearly membership fee. Membership benefits often include discounts to monthly meetings, as well as a listing in the group roster. $25 might seem a bit high, but remember that it includes lunch as well as the opportunity to meet other great business women who are eager to meet you, too.

The format is similar to networking groups. Usually the meetings are held during the lunch hour at a restaurant, starting with 15-30 minutes of gathering and informal networking, followed by each member or guest saying something about their business, followed by a featured speaker. Usually a prize raffle and announcements round out the meeting before it ends.

Bonus Tip: Call before attending your first women's group meeting. Introduce yourself and explain what you do, then ask if you can make a donation to their prize raffle. They'll happily accept.

I've donated inexpensive $10-bottles of wine, a small basket with a microfiber cloth and bottle of fragrant Mrs. Meyer's cleaner, as well as 90 minutes of free cleaning services. All have been well received.

Having your name announced during the raffle, along with seeing your fabulous donated gift, will have people smiling and nodding at you. They will be impressed that you're a guest who cared enough to take the time to donate a prize. You're making an awesome impression on a whole group of women who may want to hire you soon.

Chambers of Commerce

Your local Chamber of Commerce can be another a great place to meet other business owners. Annual membership dues can be fairly affordable or quite expensive, depending where you live. They usually include free or discounted business workshops or seminars as well as some really nice networking events.

Even if you don't join, most offer free community networking events that are open to all. The one in my area meets the first Friday of each month in the morning from 7:00-9:00 and offers free coffee and breakfast goodies.

When I first moved to my new town, I attended a couple of these morning meetings and really enjoyed them. It's a great place to walk around and meet other eager, friendly business people.

Service Organizations

Even if you can't find a nearby women's group or business networking meeting, almost every city and town has at least one service organization such as Rotary, Lions or Kiwanis.

These groups aren't specifically for business networking, but rather focus on voluntary community service. Members are passionate about developing leadership skills and building personal and business relationships.

Just don't go into one of these service groups for the sole purpose of gaining business. The purpose of these organizations is to provide needed voluntary community service, and any business that comes your way may take time and be a secondary benefit of attending meetings regularly.

A Winning Attitude

I've mentioned several times the importance of smiling, displaying a positive attitude and showing some enthusiasm for what you do.

Here's a great, true story to bring it home. I was a first-time guest at a networking meeting with a husband-and-wife team of commercial cleaners. During the entire meeting, the wife looked as though she was sucking a lemon, and the husband looked unhappy and miserable, complete with slumped shoulders. He lacked confidence and pride when he spoke. It was awkward and uncomfortable to watch.

Well, during this meeting I received 3

referrals, and I was a first-time guest! The other couple did not receive any referrals at all. Is there any wonder why?

Of course, you'll never make that mistake, because you take pride in what you do.

Now you can take that smile and winning attitude all the way to the bank!

GETTING YOUR FIRST CLIENT

You've got a Referral! Now What?

You've named your business, bought business cards and networked at two or three meetings. And then you got your first referral. Great! Now what?

Don't hesitate – act right away! Get their address and set up a time to come over to look at their house in order to prepare a quote.

Tell them that this will only take about 10 minutes.

Once you arrive, smile, shake their hand, thank them for letting you come by to take a look at their home, and then hand them a card. Pets may greet you, too, and it's good to make friends with them, assuming they're friendly.

Sometimes, clients are apologetic for the mess and almost seem paralyzed at the thought of showing you around. I always tell them, *"Your house is fine! Remember, I wouldn't be in business if everyone had a perfect house. I love to clean, so I think we've got a win-win situation here!"* They like that, and they know I'm there to help, not to judge.

Carry a clipboard with a pad of paper and a pen to take quick notes as you walk through with them. Make a note of any items you will have to clean that might take extra time, such as mirrored closet doors, plantation shutters or blinds, lots of knick-knacks or ceiling fans. Also note surfaces such as carpet, rugs, wood or tile floors, stainless steel appliances - anything to jog your memory when you go home to prepare your quote.

After you're finished looking around and are back at the front door, ask for their email address and say something like, *"Great, I'll send you a quote by this evening. Don't hesitate to call or email me if you have any questions or concerns. Thank you for showing me your home. I look forward to talking to you soon!"*

Make sure you get the quote to them

that day. I've discovered that once people actually have you come over to provide a quote, they're serious about hiring someone soon. They really want to get started, so don't make them wait for their quote. The sooner, the better.

Next, I'll show you the format I use for sending email quotes.

Congratulations, you're very close to getting your first client!

How to Send a Quote

Now that you've met with your potential client at her house, it's time to put together your quote and email it to them that day.

I keep this basic template that I copy and paste into each new email, and adjust it as necessary. Feel free to use this word for word, or modify it to suit your specific client:

Hi (Name),

It was a pleasure meeting you today! And thank you for showing me around your home.

I've worked up a bi-weekly (every other week) cleaning quote for you to include:

- Dusting, including baseboards, ceiling fans and blinds

- Vacuuming hard floor surfaces and carpeted areas, and mopping

- Cobweb removal

- Cleaning the kitchen, reducing hard water deposits, wiping down appliance exteriors, wiping down cabinetry exteriors, cleaning counter tops, cleaning the inside and out of the microwave, cleaning the floor and baseboards

- Polishing stainless steel appliances

- Cleaning bathrooms, including sinks, counters, toilets, shower/tubs, reducing hard water deposits, wiping down cabinetry exteriors as needed, and cleaning floors and baseboards

- Cleaning door handles, doors and light

switches as needed

- Trash removal

- (Does not include washing dishes, making beds, laundry, cleaning interiors of oven or refrigerator.)

A bi-weekly scheduled cleaning will be $99 per visit.

The first, or "initial cleaning," will be an extra $125 (total of $224), and I'll be there for 6 hours on the first visit. Each cleaning thereafter will be the regular $99.

This includes the use of my own cleaning products, including non-toxic Mrs. Meyer's Clean Day. I only ask that you provide a roll of paper towels each time, and your vacuum for the carpeting. I supply everything else, including cleaning and polishing agents, microfiber cloths, etc...

I've attached 6 letters of recommendation. Contact information is on each letter - feel free to reach any of them for confirmation :-)

I take great pride in my work, each and every time, and welcome any questions you may have. Keep in mind that I don't subcontract my work or bring a team of strangers into your home; you can always be confident that it's just me, The Cleanup Queen. And of course, I'm bonded and insured.

I look forward to hearing from you!

Wendy Williams

The Cleanup Queen

(my phone number)

I allow the client 3 days to get back to me. Sometimes they want to think it over or discuss it with their spouse. Then I follow up after that if I haven't heard back.

I send this email to follow up:

Hi (Name),

I sent out a cleaning quote 3 days ago and just want to make sure you received it. Let me know if you have any questions or concerns. Looking forward to hearing from you!

Wendy Williams

The Cleanup Queen

(my phone number)

Everyone is busy, and they won't mind a follow-up email or call.

They Accepted Your Quote! What's Next?

If the client emails to say they accepted your quote and are eager to begin, congratulations! Now you should email them back right away, something like this:

Hi (Name),

Terrific, I'm so pleased to begin cleaning for you!

I can begin next week on Tuesday the 18th, at 8:30 and then every two weeks thereafter. I also have an opening at 12:00 on Thursday the 20th. Which would work better for you?

Let me know ASAP so I can get you

scheduled, and then I can begin working my cleaning magic!

Wendy Williams

The Cleanup Queen

(my phone number)

If you don't get a quick response via email, follow up with a phone call.

Once they confirm the date and time, get it on your calendar, and then schedule them out for 2 months. That way, you won't accidentally put a new client in that time slot. Believe me, you won't be able to keep track of all your clients in your head. I'll go over my tips later on keeping track of clients and appointments.

Also consider sending out a reminder (email, text or phone call, depending on the client) the day before their first cleaning to remind them of your arrival the next day. They'll appreciate it.

This is just the beginning. Be prepared to get more clients soon!

Keeping In Touch With Your Clients

A big compliment I get from my clients is my good communication. They'll love this about you, too. Just take into consideration each individual client's preferred method of keeping in touch, whether it's a phone call, email or text.

Many of my clients are in their 40s-60s and prefer email. Thankfully, it's my preferred method as well.

Clients in their 70s and 80s usually prefer to receive a phone call.

And my 20- to 30-something clients almost always prefer a text message.

The best time to ask this is when they first call you or when you're at their house to take notes in preparation of a quote.

There's always a good reason to keep in touch. If you have a question or a concern after a cleaning, assuming they were gone when you were there, let them know as soon as possible.

And always communicate after the first

cleaning. Most of the time, there won't be any issues. You can tell them how great things went and that everything looks sparkling clean and that you hope they are pleased.

If you need to reschedule a cleaning, let them know as far in advance as possible, and then send a reminder a few days before the scheduled change, in case they forgot to write it down.

So just remember to communicate with them to keep them informed. I've never had anyone tell me I contacted them too much. And always stay positive in your communications.

Referral Gold: Letters of Recommendation

We can all toot our own horn and say how great we are, how honest, how reliable, how good we are at cleaning... but unless people hear it from somebody else, they're a bit skeptical.

How can we get someone else to brag about us? Besides getting in front of people at business networking meetings, the Number One thing you can do to secure new clients fast is provide letters of recommendation from your satisfied clients.

If anyone is hesitant to hire you for any reason, showing them at least one solid letter of recommendation will give them the security and confidence to give you a try.

That's why these letters are pure gold!

As soon as you've cleaned a couple of times for a pleased client, ask if they'll provide you with a letter of recommendation. Let them know you want to acquire more good clients like them and that their letter will help.

Clients will eagerly agree to do so, but they don't always follow through. Everyone is busy, and this is yet another task that takes time. Let them know it doesn't have to be lengthy, and if they could just state a few things they like about you, that would be great.

Sometimes I get very brief letters, and other times it's a really nice full-page testimonial about how wonderful I am. It's heartwarming and gratifying. But most of all, new potential clients will review these letters in a highly positive way.

I keep all my letters in a file on my computer. I attach the best 4-6 letters to my cleaning quotes that I email out.

If you don't have any letters of recommendation yet from previous employers or jobs, this would be a good time to do a few free or discounted cleanings for friends or family with the promise that they will provide a good, solid letter of recommendation for you.

So get those referral letters, provide them freely to all your potential clients, and watch your business take off!

LET THE CLEANING BEGIN!

The Cleaning Routine – Where to Start?

This is your big day to clean for your first paying client! First, don't get overwhelmed. Realize that you will get everything done, but that it will probably take longer than you anticipate. But you'll get faster and more efficient with time. Keep in mind how happy your client will be when he or she sees their sparkling home.

But where do you start? Here are some tips.

 On initial cleaning days, I always complete cobweb removal throughout the entire house first, before doing anything else. You don't want to knock down cobwebby dust on areas you've already cleaned. De-cobweb the whole house, including bathrooms, all

vents and the tops of door trim where dust accumulates quickly and thickly. I like to use a cobweb duster like the one pictured here, readily available at Home Depot or Amazon for about $10.

If you ask your clients to provide paper towels, like I do, grab those, along with a kitchen bag and your cleaning supplies before heading upstairs.

Start with the upstairs bathrooms, then do the bedrooms and everything else upstairs, including dusting, vacuuming and mopping. Then repeat the process downstairs, including the kitchen.

I've seen lots of advice about working clockwise around each room and around each floor, but I haven't managed to make that work for me. But give it a try. The idea is to clean efficiently by not having to go over an area twice that you may have missed.

Sparkling Clean Bathrooms

Before you begin, make sure you've already discussed with your client any special cleaning requirements for natural or cultured stone surfaces such as marble, granite, travertine, or specialized metals on sinks or faucets or anything typically custom or high end throughout the home. Have them provide those specialized products for you each time you clean.

Never use acidic products such as Lime-A-Way, or even vinegar, on natural stone. Also don't use any abrasive products, even Soft Scrub or scouring pads, on natural stone.

Have the client provide any special cleaning products, and – as always - read the labels and follow instructions carefully. If a client gives you a specific product to use, ask them how they use it, and then read the label yourself. Many times, a client hasn't even read the label.

Also, it's helpful to have different colored microfiber cloths to use for different areas of the house, to keep bathroom germs from getting anywhere else in the house. I buy them at Walmart, and they come in bright green, orange and yellow. I use orange in the kitchen and green in the bathroom, and yellow everywhere else.

The following advice is for average, non-specialized, non-custom finishes found in the typical household. Use your own discretion and discuss any concerns with the homeowner.

Now, put on your gloves, and let's begin!

First, turn on the fan in the bathroom or open a window for ventilation, then vacuum up the hair and dust on the bathroom floor before anything else.

Toilets then get cleaned by lightly spraying the entire exterior unit down (even underneath and on the sides and on the floor around the toilet) with Mrs. Meyer's all-purpose cleaner. I use paper towels, rather than cloth, on toilets, to keep everything sanitary.

But before wiping it down, sprinkle a little Bar Keepers Friend cleanser inside the toilet bowl and use the green heavy-duty scrubber to get it clean.

If there's a heavy buildup of hard water and other stains, grab the pumice stick, wet it in the bowl, and scrub away. This may take a few rounds of scrubbing, especially if the water is hard.

Beware that the pumice stick should only be used on the inside of the bowl, not anywhere else! It sounds awful when you scrub, like you're ruining the inside finish of the bowl, but you're not. The highly toxic, acid toilet bowl cleaners everyone uses is what actually ruins the inside finish, causing stains to subsequently accumulate rapidly.

Flush, and then wipe the whole exterior of the toilet that you've pre-sprayed with a couple paper towels, starting at the top of the tank, down to the sides and base and around the floor of the toilet. Throw your used paper towels in the trash bag you brought up. Never flush paper towels.

Use the toothbrush or little small detail cleaning brush to get around the hinges and crevices, if necessary. Make sure the entire toilet is clean, inside and out, every nook and cranny and around the base of the toilet. Take extra care with toilets, because customers really notice this.

Remember to place the pumice stick, the green scouring pad and detail brush in a separate container or section of your caddy after each use, to prevent it from contaminating anything else.

Next are the sinks. On the faucets, very carefully spray on a small amount of Lime-A-Way and rinse after about 30 seconds. If the build-up is heavy, you may need to repeat this step several times, using a non-abrasive scouring pad. This helps remove and keep away hard water deposits.

Be very careful with Lime-A-Way, as it's an acid and can ruin a surface after it sits for just 1 minute. Don't spray vigorously, getting it all over the counter or mirror. I use my gloved hand behind the spray to keep the solution right where I need it. Rinse thoroughly.

Again, make sure you fully understand how to use Lime-A-Way or any acid-based cleaner properly.

Use a small amount of Soft Scrub with the blue non-abrasive scrubber on sinks. If it's a fiberglass tub or washroom sink with no previous damage, use a LA's Totally Awesome and a dampened microfiber cloth to wipe it down and then rinse and dry. If the surface is damaged (looks dull or scratched instead of glossy or shiny), use Soft Scrub.

Use the non-ammonia glass cleaner for

the mirrors and a spritz of Mrs. Meyer's with a microfiber cloth for the countertops, and then dry and polish everything off with paper towels.

In my opinion, tub and shower enclosures are the most difficult items in a house to clean. Most people don't squeegee the glass or wipe it down after each use, and the hard water, mixed with sticky soap products and body oils, causes a very hard-to-clean, damaging and unsightly film to glass, tile, grout and fiberglass.

For showers with a glass enclosure, lay a towel down outside the glass door, and then carefully step in and close the door/s. Spray a little Lime-A-Way on the interior glass walls or doors, and then quickly use a non-abrasive blue scrubber to spread around the solution. Work fast, and then completely rinse it off within 1 minute.

If the shower doesn't have a removable, hand-held shower head, rinsing can be tricky. In that case, you may get a little wet as you hold your plastic rinse cup up to the shower head to collect water for rinsing.

If the tub or shower enclosure is fiberglass, does it look dull or shiny? If it's dull or scratched, use a little Soft Scrub. If it's still shiny and new, spray it with LA's Totally Awesome to break up the oils and film before wiping it down. Rinse and then dry everything with a microfiber cloth, followed by a wipe-down with glass cleaner on the glass to make it sparkle. Make sure to clean the tracks thoroughly, too.

After you've emptied the waste basket and cleaned everything, finish up with a spray of Mrs. Meyer's cleaner on the floor and hand wipe it down, including the baseboards, with a microfiber cloth. I do this step by hand, if the bathroom is small. If it's big, you can use your mop.

Ah, there's nothing like a sparkling clean bathroom!

Gleaming Kitchens

Here's where you'll love the LA's Totally Awesome cleaner, because it devours grease and grime unlike anything else. Use it on the microwave interior, on the stove, light switches and extra-gunky spots on the kitchen floor.

I dilute mine 50/50 with water in a spray bottle, but I also keep a bottle of full-strength solution out in my car in case the job is extra heavy-duty. Again, read the directions carefully and make sure the room is well ventilated.

On stove tops and the inside of microwave ovens (except on the microwave door), spray and let sit for 2 or 3 minutes before wiping down. On the inside of the microwave door, just spray a little on your microfiber cloth first and then wipe down so that the cleaning solution doesn't ruin the special plastic film on the interior door.

Use the non-ammonia glass cleaner and a clean terry cloth after you've done a thorough cleaning of the microwave and stove, to leave everything sparkling.

My favorite stainless steel cleaner is by Sprayway. I don't use it to clean, however. Clean all kitchen stainless steel with LA's Totally Awesome and a damp microfiber cloth and let dry. Then follow with Sprayway Stainless Steel Cleaner and a terry cloth for a perfectly clean, glowing finish.

Even black enamel stove tops look great with Sprayway Stainless Steel Cleaner.

A tablespoon or so of Mrs. Meyers or Fabuloso added to about a gallon of water can be used to mop the floors with your microfiber mop head.

Next to a sparkling bathroom, there's nothing like a gleaming kitchen!

Final Cleaning Tips

- After the de-cobwebbing, bathrooms and kitchen are finished, you can dust, vacuum large area rugs and carpeting, then vacuum all hard floors, followed by mopping and taking out the trash and recyclables.

- If possible, try to vacuum your way out of a room. If the carpeting is plush, clients don't like to see your footprints left behind.

- Ask your client if they like a strong scent left behind after you've cleaned. Some of my clients don't like strong fragrances and prefer my unscented or minimally scented products. But lately, I've had more requests to use something fragrant on the floor. I've been using Fabuloso for mopping which leaves a long-lasting scent behind, and they love it. Just ask what they prefer.

- Be careful to place items back where they belong. This is another pet-peeve of many clients. Most people don't mind if an item is moved a little, but they don't like it when you completely clear the counter, table or desk and forget where things go. They don't want to rearrange everything when they get home.

- Make sure that any windows or doors you've opened are securely closed and locked before you leave.

- Don't let pets get into your supplies or get out the door!

- Last, make sure you DOUBLE check that the door is locked securely as you leave.

Your clients will really appreciate knowing you've cleaned their home thoroughly and with care!

What I Won't Clean

 Here are a few things you may want to consider, but it's totally up to you and the level of service you wish to provide.

In my quote, I always outline precisely what I will clean. Still, some clients want me to do extra, even though they agreed to my terms. When I started my cleaning business, I would do what they asked, afraid they might not continue my services if I declined.

Now I politely but gently state that I don't clean certain items. But if they want me to do special cleaning tasks on a separate day, I'd be happy to do that for my minimum charge of $115 for 3 hours of cleaning, working down their cleaning task priority list.

Here's a list of the tasks I don't tackle as part of a regular cleaning, and something you may want to consider, too:

- Stain removal on rugs, carpeting,

furniture or upholstery.

- Cleaning dishes. I ask that dishes be put away before I arrive.

- Washing windows. But I will clean the inside of the window above the kitchen sink.

- Doing laundry.

- Making beds.

- Cleaning oven interior.

- Cleaning refrigerator interior.

- Cleaning blinds. I dust them, but don't clean them.

- Picking up or cleaning pet feces or urine, and I don't change litter boxes.

Sometimes a client will ask me about these things when I'm looking at their home in preparation of giving a quote, and I'll say, *"Oh, I'm sorry, I don't clean windows, but I have the names of two excellent window washers in this area,"* or *"I'm sorry, I don't actually clean the blinds, but I will make sure they're dusted. I have the name of a company that will clean them, and then I can keep them looking nice with regular dusting."* Usually they're fine with this.

When elderly people call to inquire about my services, I ask them if they're looking for help with beds, laundry and dishes, and they usually are.

So if anyone really wants me to include these chores as part of their regular service, I let them know that I don't provide those services and that they might be happier with a maid service instead. A maid service, usually a large corporate residential cleaning company, is more inclined to do these tasks as part of their routine. They have teams of workers who tackle these tasks more quickly and efficiently than a solo operator.

If you decide, however, to include some of these things in your routine cleanings, please charge accordingly. Cleaning blinds or the inside of an oven, for instance, can take a very long time.

Most people would love to have a full

maid service but don't want to pay the expensive fee. They're usually more than happy having you do the routine cleaning chores.

The Lemon-Scented Truth about Green Cleaning

Thankfully, people are more aware of their environment these days. You'll find that many new clients will ask if you use non-toxic ingredients.

I truthfully answer, *"I always use the least toxic product for the job, and I include non-toxic Mrs. Meyer's Clean Day."*

The reality is that if you only used only non-toxic, "natural," or homemade cleaners in your business, you wouldn't get anything very clean after hours of scrubbing, and neither you nor your clients would be happy with the results.

Most "green" all-purpose cleaners are

mostly water with a small amount of fragrance and vegetable-based cleaner. They are minimally effective and smell nice, but the water and your microfiber cloth is doing most of the real cleaning, not the product. And that's fine for cleaning lightly dirty surfaces.

But you can't use that on grease-laden stove tops and microwave interiors caked with blown up bits of dried, crusty pizza sauce and cheese, for instance. You also can't use that on the inside of a toilet bowl. Further, you can't use that to get hard water buildup off of glass shower doors and faucets, no matter how much you scrub. It's chemistry, and certain products don't work on certain messes, period.

I have to smile when I see all the homemade concoctions people use such as toothpaste, peanut butter, hydrogen peroxide, baking soda and essential oils. These things have a little value, but not very much. As a professional cleaner, you can't rely on these formulas.

So what's a house cleaner to do? You need to keep an arsenal of products that work best for each job and let you clean up with the least amount of scrubbing and the least amount of product, not only saving you time, but saving the item being cleaned from excessive scratching and scrubbing, and also using the least amount of product necessary. It's the best way to clean "naturally"!

This isn't trickery or deceit. You're letting your client know the truth without getting into an argument about chemistry or the negative effects of ineffective cleaning methods and products.

If a client has specific medical needs, they'll let you know exactly what can or can't be used in the house. For instance, some clients with asthma don't like to use ammonia products such as Windex. I don't use them either, but the point is that they'll let you know.

I've been asked this question about

non-toxic products a hundred times. My clients are always happy with the cleanings because I'm using the correct – and therefore minimal amount of - product for each job. Your clients will be happy with you, too.

STAYING ORGANIZED

Keeping Track of Clients

 There are so many modern ways to keep track of everything these days. But I'll share my very simple method. Use whatever you like, as long as you can refer to it every day.

This is old school, but I use ruled index cards to keep track of all my clients. I list their name, phone, address, email, preferred method of communication, and even directions to their house. I also list their pets and kids names, which is important when you're just starting out.

I bring the index card with me in my car every time I visit their house, just in case I need to make a note after a cleaning. I don't rely on my memory, because after you've cleaned for 2-6 hours, you're tired. I bring the cards in at the end of each day and see if there are any notes about concerns I need to bring up to the client that evening.

I also enter in the names and phone numbers of my clients into my phone. Occasionally there's a situation where I need to call the client upon arriving at their house. One time, the client's big dog was out wandering the street, and I had to call to ask if I could bring him in. Another time, the garage door code didn't work, and they had to come home from work to fix it (the battery was dead).

The downside to keeping everything electronically in your phone, for instance, is if you lose or break the device. I keep info in my phone, too, but the complete record of my client is on paper for this reason. Paper is a great backup to electronic storage. Plus it's easy to make changes.

Keeping Track of Appointments

Once you secure your first client, it's critical to keep track of appointments on a calendar of some sort.

Again, I'm old school and prefer paper and pencil. The method doesn't matter, as long as you make note of who is scheduled when. I keep a calendar of appointments out by 2 to 3 months.

I use the free, printable monthly calendars by calendarlabs.com and print out the year on regular 8 ½ by 11 paper. I make small pencil notations of my clients' appointments in the daily squares. It works for me, but use whatever you're used to or feel comfortable with.

You might want to use an app on your smart phone or an online calendar. But beware, if you lose your phone or your computer crashes, you're in trouble. I never lose my paper calendar, and that's partly why I prefer it. Plus I can make quick changes since it's written in pencil.

Keeping Track of Keys and Codes

Most of my clients provide a house key, and I let them know that I keep it on my ring, unmarked. That way, in case I lost

the keys, no one would ever be able to identify the house to which the key belongs. But I'm quick to let them know that I've never lost my keys in my life.

You may want to keep your own personal keys on a separate ring, but that's up to you. I keep two separate rings of keys – one for clients, one for personal - that are hooked together. That way, I have them all together, but they're on two separate rings for easy identification.

I just visually memorize the key to the client, but you may want to use a color-coded tab for each client's key to make it easier.

Some clients have gate codes or garage door codes or house alarm codes. It's very important that you list your client's alarm or gate or garage code in a "hidden" way on their information card, just in case it got into the hands of anyone other than you.

On my index card with the client's information, I list a long string of numbers and symbols on the bottom of the card, and within that string is the actual code. I don't list it as "Code" either.

For instance, you'd see something like this: "1#187785*4470#90009*7" but only I know that the code starts the fifth character from the left, or the third from the right and ends with a particular symbol.

In this example, you might want to identify your code starting with the fifth character from the left and ending with an asterisk, so the actual code would be (marked in bold here): 1#18**7785***4470#90009*7.

Just keep your method consistent with each client so you don't confuse yourself.

Develop your own secret way of identifying codes so that they stay safe and unidentifiable to anyone but you.

Also, ask your client for instructions on what to do if you punch in an incorrect number. Each alarm system is different.

One time, I accidentally hit a wrong number and couldn't clear it to start over, setting off the alarm. It was loud and embarrassing, and then the police came, and then the client. That mess could have been avoided if we had just gone over what to do beforehand.

SAFETY FIRST

Keeping You and Your Clients Safe

Safety is a big concern on each and every job. And I'm not only talking about safety of the client's belongings, but your personal safety.

First off, always wear protective gloves while "wet" cleaning. I rarely get sick, despite cleaning many toilets and sick houses every week, because I keep gloves on my hands and keep my hands away from my face. The only time I don't wear gloves is while dusting and vacuuming.

I've tried different brands of gloves. The longer the wear and more comfortable they are, the more expensive. But I'd rather pay a buck fifty more to get the nice latex gloves which are more comfortable and that last a week or longer as opposed to the super cheap variety that aren't as comfortable and break in a day or two. My favorites are Playtex Living Gloves that cost about $2.85 per pair.

Always be deliberate and aware of your surroundings. Try to push your supplies off to the side whenever possible, so that you and your clients don't trip over them.

Elbows: This sounds funny, but you need to watch your elbow, especially when you're vacuuming or mopping your way around and out of a room. French doors, glass-doored hutches and grandfather clocks, when met with your flying elbow, can spell disaster. Be careful!

Also, make sure you have good rubber-soled shoes on. Beware, though, that when you're mopping ceramic tile floors, they become slick as ice, and you need to move very slowly and cautiously.

I suggest you don't use ladders, either. If you need a boost, bring along a small 1-2-foot step stool, or ask the client if they have one you can use. Lots of clients have big, tall furniture, and you might need a boost to dust the top. I also use an extension pole with a cobweb brush to reach high cobwebs and to clean ceiling fans.

Decide if you can move or lift heavy furniture and only agree to do so if you can do it safely. I move some furniture but am careful to protect my back. Sometimes a client will ask if I can help them move furniture so I can vacuum underneath, and that works out well. Otherwise, I use the slim attachment on my canister vacuum to reach underneath and around difficult-to-reach places.

Cleaning When Your Clients Are Home

More and more of my clients are self-employed, working in a home office, or they have young children at home. My biggest concern is their safety, especially after I've mopped.

Whenever I'm near where they're working, I always let them know, *"Be careful, I've got my supplies right here!"*

That just lets them know to watch out, even though I do my best to set things to the side as I go.

And I never, ever neglect to let them know I'm about to mop. I always say, *"Be really careful, I don't want you to trip on the wet floor, it's super slick!"* They are appreciative of the warning, because they don't want to take a tumble.

First-Aid Kit

Even though you're careful, cuts and nicks and other small mishaps occur occasionally. It's a good idea to keep a small, inexpensive safety kit in your car.

Bandages and antibiotic cream are the two most important items to have on hand, if nothing else. If your finger gets nicked and starts bleeding, wash and bandage it right away.

Cleaning Around Pets

Most pets are naturally curious about your cleaning supplies, and they may want to sniff and even grab something, which can be dangerous. Cleaning products are toxic to pets!

To the curious dog, your cleaning caddy and bucket are full of toys and fun things to "play" with.

One time I had to chase down a dog that nabbed a piece of steel wool from my caddy, and I had to grab it from his mouth right before he swallowed it! That would have been disastrous. Lesson learned.

If Fido is snooping near your supplies, either shut the door to the room you're cleaning to keep him out or put him outside or in another room, with your client's permission.

I absolutely love cats and dogs, and most of them love me. Talking to and petting my clients' furry friends gives me great joy.

But every once in a while, you might find that someone's pet just doesn't like you for whatever reason (just like people). Just take it slow and don't try to force the friendship. Animals may bite when they're scared or nervous.

Ask your client if you can bring a couple of small treats when you arrive. This usually does the trick for me.

Safety first for you and for the animals.

Getting Calls from Weirdos

Your cards may get passed around to people you've never met. Referrals are great, and you'll be happy that word of mouth is spreading.

But I've had several men (and women) call me who couldn't tell me who referred them, and they spoke unclearly and just sounded a bit strange. Perhaps they were legitimate, but I felt uncomfortable and told them I wasn't taking on new clients. Use your own good judgment; if you feel uncomfortable, pass on the client.

If you'd like to meet the client at their home to give a quote, you can always let them know that you'll be bringing your spouse or friend to "take notes" while you're there. It's always best to use caution and protect yourself.

At the very least, no matter who you're visiting, always let your spouse, or a friend or family member know when you're heading out to anyone's house to give a quote for the first time. Jot down the person's name, address and phone number and approximately when you'll be back.

Always use good, common sense to protect your safety.

MORE MONEY MATTERS

How and When to Raise Your Rates

 Most women worry at the thought of raising their rates, because they fear their clients will be upset and discontinue services.

I've only had one client do that, and I was fine with letting her go. I understood her position, but she received a great rate for a year. It was time to raise my rates equal to those of my new client rates.

Some clients might be getting a great rate because I underestimated how long the cleaning would take each visit. In these cases, I raise the rate after 6 months.

Sometimes, the circumstances change in the household, and the rates need to be adjusted accordingly, and right away.

Here are a few things I've encountered that sometimes warranted a rate increase:

- Adding a significant amount of furniture and decorative items (more dusting)

- Number of permanent adult household members increased

- Adding blinds to windows where there were none (blinds take time to dust)

- Removing carpeting and adding hard surface flooring (requiring mopping)

- Adding pets. (This varies. One client had a huge Bull Mastiff that shed what seemed to be a pound of fur a week. Other clients have 2 dogs that hardly shed at all. Also consider if they are indoor/outdoor pets, which bring in a great deal of mud and dirt year-round.)

Here is a sample of an email I've sent when asking for a rate increase:

Hi (Name),

I sure enjoy cleaning for you, and I hope you continue to be pleased as well. I love how your home looks so sparkling clean when I leave!

You are a valued client, and I hope to continue on with you for a long time.

After thoughtful consideration, I've decided to raise my rates a bit due to the increased time it takes to clean because of the (explain what's changed).

Starting (date), the rate will go from $89 to $99.

I hope you understand and feel it's fair.

Please call or email me with any questions or concerns. I want to make sure you're happy.

In the meantime, have a wonderful week, and I'll see you on (date).

Thank you!

Wendy Williams

The Cleanup Queen

(my phone number)

It can be difficult to raise your rates, but remember that you're being fair and providing good value for your service. If you're doing everything right, they'll probably stay with you.

Remember this is your business, and you can charge what you think is fair. I judge this on an individual basis. I don't charge all of my clients the same rate. Some clients are such a joy to work for and have really easy houses to clean. I'll keep their rates lower even if I have to drive an extra distance or deal with extra cleaning tasks.

Collecting Money

I ask my clients to put the check somewhere obvious, such as on the kitchen counter.

Occasionally, a client will forget to leave your check. So far, I've never had a client refuse to pay. But if they forget, I simply send an email or leave a voice mail message right away.

Here's my voice mail message:

Hi (Name). This is Wendy, The Cleanup Queen, and I just wanted to let you know that everything went great today!

I didn't see a check on the counter, but I know you're super busy. Could you just drop it in the mail today or tomorrow at (my Post Office Box address)? Thanks, and let me know if you have any questions. Have a great day!

Sometimes they'll still forget to drop it in the mail in a timely manner, so just send another reminder. It's always worked for me, so give it a try.

DIFFICULT SITUATIONS

Difficult Clients

 Thankfully, I've had just a few difficult clients to deal with, and I want to share with you what I've learned from these experiences so that it will help you deal with yours.

Let's take them on a case-by-case basis. The names here are changed to protect the "difficult."

I met Mindy at a women's networking group and was happy to have her as a client. But from day one, the complaints began: The blinds weren't dusted enough, there was a speck of dirt in the corner, the floor wasn't clean enough, I wasn't using the right amount of cleaner on the wood floors, and why wasn't I cleaning her toothbrush cup? One day, she even handed me a jar of paste wax and asked me to hand polish and buff her wood bed. That alone would have been an extra hour of work, which was not outlined in her original quote, but I did it anyway.

I did the extra work, and I apologized each time she complained that something wasn't right, and said I'd work extra hard on the item/s on the next visit. But still, the complaints kept coming.

I am eager to please, but eventually I realized there was no pleasing this woman, and eventually I dreaded cleaning for her. I also didn't want to face her when I knew it was time to let her go. Instead, I emailed her, stating that I would no longer travel to her town to clean, because it was just too far.

That was not a good way to handle it. First, I wasn't being truthful; I actually didn't want to face her. Second, what if she hadn't been far away? I couldn't have used that excuse.

Now I would call her - not send an email - and explain that we're probably not a good fit since I can't seem to resolve her ongoing complaints. I'd then go on to apologize that it didn't work out and that I would happily clean for her one last time so that she'd have time to find a replacement cleaner.

Now let's talk about Esther. Esther was just always intense and cranky. One day I had to cancel her cleaning appointment because I was sick (very rare for me) and she huffed and puffed and complained about how inconvenient that was for her. I didn't appreciate her attitude and subtle accusation that I was lying about being sick, and I told her so. I finished by stating I wouldn't be coming back and quickly hung up the phone.

Again, I wouldn't recommend that response because it was unprofessional on my part.

I was emotionally charged, hurt, and acted hastily. I should have let her finish her complaining, and then calmly state that I understood her position, but that I would happily reschedule her visit, even if I had to come in on a weekend. Isn't hindsight 20/20?

Bev was a busy business owner whose house was quite cluttered. Piles everywhere and a real challenge to clean properly. But I cleaned for her every other week, and all seemed to be going well. But she kept forgetting to leave her payments out for me, and then the checks would bounce. After the third time of getting a bad check, I told her I wouldn't be able to continue cleaning for her.

She made good on the checks, but I still let her go. I felt I handled that situation well, in a professional manner.

Last, let's talk about Debbie. I loved cleaning for her, as she was happy and so appreciative of my services. However, after about a year's time, the cancelations began to occur more frequently, leaving me without a job to fill in, and I was losing income.

Because I got her house clean and in

order, she just didn't need me as much since she wanted to keep up the maintenance herself. So I handled it the right way by asking her if she didn't mind my cleaning for her on an as-needed basis instead. She seemed relieved, and we were both happy.

So treat your clients well, always do your best work, stay honest and communicative, and you'll have very few complaints. But life isn't perfect, and you'll get a complainer now and then. If you dread the job, it's time to move on.

Be honest and understanding of their situation, and you may continue to get referrals from them in the future.

Cancelations

In 6 years of cleaning, only one client has canceled excessively on me. This is subjective, of course, but I'd say that more than two cancelations in six months is too much.

Now, sometimes clients call at least several days or even weeks ahead to let me know they'll be on vacation, for instance. That's fine, because you might be able to fill in another client in their time slot.

But when clients call the night before a schedule cleaning – or worse, on the way to their cleaning – make a note of it and begin keeping track. You just have to make sure it won't become a habit because the client is feeling a financial pinch or because they just don't want to prepare the house for your arrival.

Remember, you're losing out on that income whenever someone cancels. If your schedule isn't full, you might be able to reschedule them. If you can't do that, you're out of luck until the next cleaning.

But that's part of what I accept, and I don't charge a cancelation fee. However, if it ever becomes an issue for you, I would communicate with the client that perhaps they would like you to clean on an as-needed basis. Or maybe they want to continue on as usual, but you will charge $20 the next time that 36 hours' notice isn't given.

Lockouts

Sometimes clients leave a key for me in a hiding place, but I've been locked out a couple of times when they forgot. Again, I don't have a formal policy on lockouts, but if it becomes a problem, you may want to charge $20-$40 per incident.

Services Guide

Some people like to have everything spelled out at the beginning, so they know where they stand. I've experimented with creating a "Services Guide" which is a formal, written set of expectations that your client agrees to before you begin.

I never finished it, because I know I would be uncomfortable if I had to point to it if a problem arose, saying, *"See, you agreed to this."* No, I would rather just discuss it with the client or let them go. You won't produce quality work if you're resentful or feel like a doormat.

Having said that, a Services Guide would be a written document that could be very helpful and outline any of following:

- Your contact information

- List of services you provide

- List of services you do not include

- Cancelation policy

- Lockout policy

- Payment requirements

- Returned checks (non-sufficient funds) and fees collected

- Special instructions or requirements of the client that you agree to

You can attach the Services Guide when you email your quote, and/or print a copy and leave it for them at the initial cleaning.

When Something Breaks

Despite being careful on every job, sometimes things break. Usually it's because a decorative item was previously broken and not glued back together well; when you pick it up, it falls apart.

I've accidentally knocked something off a shelf, holding my breath as I watched it – seemingly in slow motion - plummet to the ground and break into pieces.

How do you handle these mishaps?

Carefully pick the pieces up and put them on a paper towel, and then set that on a counter where it will be easily seen when they come home.

As soon as possible, right after the cleaning, email or call the client to let them know what happened and that you are sorry. I even offer to pay for the item, although no one has taken me up on it yet, and they usually feel sorry that I feel so bad.

Recently, I clearly wasn't thinking when I used a scouring pad on a shower mirror that was suctioned onto the wall. These kinds of mirrors are not glass, but plastic, and I scratched it up. Now I know better.

I left $20 on their counter and called my client, explaining what had happened. I said if the replacement mirror cost more than $20 to let me know, and I would be happy to pay it. He said I didn't need to leave the money at all and that everything was fine. I knew he appreciated the gesture, though.

Always be careful. But if something does happen, promptly and thoroughly explain the situation, and sincerely apologize several times and offer to pay for a replacement. My experience has shown that most people don't mind much and quickly forget it. They'll just be happy you do such a good job cleaning for them and that you were honest about the mishap –

and that you communicated quickly.

FINAL WORDS

Are you now feeling excited, motivated and ready to start your own cleaning business?

You have everything you need here to take action now!

I can't think of a more low-cost, in-demand business – in any economy - that can be started as quickly as house cleaning. You can begin to provide value for others while fulfilling your own dreams of freedom and living life on your own terms.

I hope my enthusiasm and love of this business has inspired you to get started so you can create your own success story.

Remember, you can reach me at wendiki@sbcglobal.net. Happy Cleaning!

Wendy Williams

"The Cleanup Queen"

www.TheCleanupQueen.com

Made in the USA
Charleston, SC
03 February 2016